How to survive and succeed as a Teaching Assistant

Veronica Birkett

How to survive and succeed as a Teaching Assistant

LL01513

ISBN 1 85503 342 9

© Author Veronica Birkett

Illustrated by Rebecca Barnes

All rights reserved

First published 2001

Revised 2002

LDA, Duke Street, Wisbech, Cambs PE13 2AE

3195 Wilson Drive, Grand Rapids, MI 49544, USA

Contents

Contents

Who
will
benefit
from this
book?

Who will benefit from this book?

This book has been written for Teaching Assistants and, in many respects, by Teaching Assistants (TAs). The book will also benefit heads and teachers who want to work more effectively with TAs.

The author would like to thank the TAs who helped to write the book. These include Pat Stockley of Little London School in Willenhall, West Midlands; Karen Hudson of New Invention Infants School, also in Willenhall; and Stephanie Massey of Rushall JMI School, Walsall.

The author would also like to thank the following:

- All of the TAs who have attended training sessions and kindly took the time to complete questionnaires regarding their role.
- Her 'secretary' Di Davies, for her expertise on the computer and comforting presence in times of need.
- Tim Hazledine of Walsall Learning Support Service, who years ago employed her as a member of his team, giving her both the opportunity to learn a great deal about teaching pupils with SEN and the privilege of meeting and working with TAs.

About
the author

About the author

Veronica Birkett is a writer and freelance educational consultant. She is also a very experienced trainer, an OFSTED inspector and, above all, a teacher who still regularly works in schools supporting special needs provision. Her books include *How to Survive and Succeed as a SENCo in the Primary School*, published by LDA.

Veronica is willing to visit your school to provide a one-day training session for your TAs. You have a choice of three courses:

- Behaviour management for TAs
- The role of the TA
- Teaching literacy to pupils with special educational needs.

If you are interested, and would like further information, you will find Veronica's web site at www.sen-services.com, or you may phone 01543 255335.
For extra copies of this book please call LDA on 01945 463441.

Chapter 1
How Teaching Assistants came to be

Ten years ago, the responsibilities of today's TAs were very poorly defined. Occasional 'classroom assistants' or 'ancillaries' were employed in schools, usually to help with general classroom management and only occasionally with the support of the child. Classroom assistants required no training and had no official job description. Had there been such a thing, it might have looked like this.

Job description

Willing, cheerful and hard-working person required to:

Put up wall displays and take down wall displays

Make and deliver cups of tea at specified times to teachers

Wash up cups of said teachers

Mix paints

Clean up pupils after accidents – stick plasters on to cuts

Carry out playground duties

Ring the bell

Tidy out the art cupboard

Remove staples from display board

Hear pupils read, again and again and again, and again

It was a pleasant enough job. It usually fitted in with looking after the classroom assistants' own children, was convenient and gave a measure of job satisfaction. The usual procedure in schools was to divide the time of the classroom assistants between all the teachers, who would look forward to their 'Mrs Cannybody' time, even if it were for no more than one hour a week. It was the 1993 Education Act, followed by the introduction of the Code of Practice on the identification and assessment of special educational needs (SEN) in 1994, that introduced significant changes in the number, status and work of classroom assistants.

The introduction of a National Curriculum for all schools following the Education Reform Act of 1988 had a radical effect on general classroom practice. So did the 1994 Code of Practice on the identification and assessment of pupils with SEN. Like the National Curriculum, the Code of Practice introduced a national framework. It provided guidance for schools in making appropriate provision for pupils with SEN. This is where the role of the TA as we know it today originates.

Schools employ TAs for different reasons. Every school should have two separate job descriptions, one for TAs who have a general role of support and the other for those who are employed specifically to work with pupils with SEN. The job description is very important. It clarifies what the school expects TAs to do. It is a form of agreement. When you take on the role, it is the particular duties outlined in your job description that you are agreeing to. If further duties are requested which you are not happy with and which are not included in the job description, you have the right to refuse to carry them out.

Job description for TA (general duties)

Purpose

To work with and support members of the teaching staff in ensuring that pupils receive the highest possible standards of care and education, becoming safe, secure and successful.

Duties

Working within established guidelines to support the teacher in:

- ensuring that pupils are safe;
- teaching the planned curriculum;
- effectively using resources;
- producing and maintaining a welcoming and stimulating classroom environment;
- encouraging pupils to work and play independently;
- evaluating and planning children's work;
- maintaining strong home/school links.

The TA should also:

- be involved in planning and taking the initiative to ensure that the lesson objective is understood before teaching begins;
- evaluate designated teaching activities and feed back to class teacher;
- assist in national and school-based assessments arrangements, e.g. baseline, SATs, ALS.
- meet regularly with class teachers to plan work and raise/resolve concerns.

Job description for TAs employed to work with pupils with SEN or statements

Main responsibilities

To support named children who are protected by a statement of SEN or who are in need of additional support owing to learning or other difficulties.

To work under the guidance of the Special Educational Needs Co-ordinator (SENCo), head teacher and respective class teachers.

Special conditions

The TA will be made aware of the relevant contents of the statement of SEN, if a pupil has one.

The TA will be familiar with the pupil's Individual Education Plan.

Main functions

To minister to the physical needs of the child with reference to guidance on first aid in schools and the school policy on the administration of medicines.

To support the child in all areas of the curriculum, as directed by the class teacher.

To support the child as a member of a collaborative group.

To help the child develop both social and organisational skills.

To monitor the child's work and keep appropriate records.

To carry out specific programmes of work devised to meet the child's specific needs.

To assist in the planning of relevant activities to attain the above functions.

To prepare appropriate materials.

To liaise with parents and professionals.

To work within the general aims of the school, and to contribute to the overall ethos of the school.

To undertake any related activities appropriate to working with the special needs child as directed by the head teacher/ SENCo.

What is a statement?

Pupils with statements have been recognised by Local Education Authorities (LEAs) as needing extra support in order to benefit from mainstream education. A statement is a document which declares the intention of the LEA to provide special equipment (if required) and financial aid to schools to employ a TA or, if appropriate, a teacher to work with pupils deemed vulnerable and in need of support to maintain their place in a mainstream school. The statementing process is a very long and expensive one for LEAs to undertake.

In 1998 the government's Programme for Action underlined their drive to include more pupils with SEN in mainstream schools, with support. As a result of this inclusion policy some special schools and units have closed. The drive towards including most pupils with SEN in mainstream schools continues and with it the job opportunities for TAs.

FOOD FOR THOUGHT

Make a difference

The current demand for adult literacy classes is a sad reflection on how many schools in the past failed to address the problems of their SEN pupils. Many left school without learning to read, write or spell. This has a powerfully negative effect on a person's quality of life. The TA's input can make the difference between a person learning to read or not.

Afterthought

This chapter acknowledges the passing of 'Mrs Cannybody'. Many teachers miss her comforting presence. I would personally like to thank all those classroom assistants who helped me transform children's artwork into wonderful displays; cleaned up unmentionable messes in my classroom; brought me cups of tea on cold, cheerless mornings; and comforted me in times of stress with soothing words, encouragement and kindness.

Thank you.

See Appendix at the back of this book for more on the history of education for children with special needs.

Chapter 2
How do we decide whether a child has special needs?

Under the 1994 SEN Code of Practice the government suggested schools should follow a five-stage process. The process operated if a teacher became concerned about a particular child. The teacher may have observed the pupil struggling with their work. Poor test results – for example in baseline assessments, SATs at the end of Key Stages 1 and 2 and other school tests – may have reinforced these observations. After consultation with the SENCo the pupil would be placed on the school SEN register at stage 1 and the parents informed. The official process then began.

A child with mild difficulties would remain on the register for only a short time, additional monitoring and differentiation of the curriculum by the class teachers usually proving effective.

Pupils with more profound problems would progress through stage 2, when they would work towards targets on an individual education plan (IEP). They may then be placed at stage 3, when the LEA would provide the support of an outside professional. To be placed at stage 4 meant the LEA would provide a statutory assessment to decide if a pupil needed a statement.

Changes

The year 2002 saw the introduction of a revised Code of Practice into schools. The old five-stage process was abandoned. Identification of pupils with SEN now begins with School Action, which follows consultation between the teacher, parent and SENCo and leads to an IEP being devised. The pupil's work is monitored and parents are encouraged to work with the child at home. The IEP is reviewed at least twice a year. Parents must always be invited to these reviews. TAs may be involved at this stage. If the pupil fails to make progress despite school action, the school will apply to the LEA to move onto School Action Plus. If the LEA decides this is appropriate, a visiting professional will offer advice to the school regarding the targets on the IEP and will usually monitor the pupil's progress. Various outside professionals may become involved, drawn from the following list:

- ⊙ Educational Psychology Service
- ⊙ Learning Support Service
- ⊙ Behaviour Support Service

There is a destiny that makes us brothers: none goes his way alone. All that we send into the lives of others, comes back into our own.

Edwin Markham

- Hearing Impaired Service
- Visual Impaired Service
- Speech and Language Therapy Service
- Pre-school Service
- Hospital Teaching Service
- Clinical psychologists
- Child psychiatrists
- Paediatricians
- Personnel from the health authority and social services
- Education Welfare Officer
- Occupational therapists
- Physiotherapists.

In some cases, more than one professional may be involved with a child, as in the case of Lucy.

CASE STUDY

Lucy

Lucy was developing hearing difficulties as well as learning difficulties. Despite the fact that Lucy had an IEP providing School Action and her work had been regularly reviewed, she was falling further and further behind the rest of the class and becoming increasingly frustrated. When a test confirmed deteriorating hearing, the school applied to the LEA for Lucy to be placed at School Action Plus. They requested that a member of the Learning Support Service (made up of peripatetic teachers employed by the LEA) should carry out an assessment of her learning difficulties and that a member of the Hearing Impaired Service should also assess her needs. The LEA decided this would be of benefit, the professional assessments were made and an IEP was drawn up.

Early intervention

At School Action Plus some LEAs provide financial support, which is often used to employ a TA on a short-term contract to support the pupil. This is becoming customary as it is clearly of benefit to the pupil to receive support promptly rather than waiting for receipt of a statement. It helps the teacher, who may be finding it difficult to cope single-handedly, with a pupil's particular difficulties. Parents find early intervention reassuring. Early intervention also benefits the LEA, as it reduces the possibility of a child needing a statement later and cuts down on costs.

Most pupils who receive this support make sufficient progress and do not go on to need a statement. However, there will always be children with a difficulty or disability who, without the security of regular support and access to

You give but little when you give of your possessions. It is when you give of yourself that you truly give

Kahlil Gibran

on-going professional advice, would not be able to stay in school. For these reasons schools, with the agreement of the parents, may make a request to the LEA to make a statutory assessment. It is estimated that one child in fifty may need this type of assessment. Parents also have the right to request the assessment even though the school may not think such a course of action is appropriate. The LEA has twenty-nine days from the time they receive the request in which to decide if an assessment is to be made. If they agree to assess they have twelve weeks to decide whether a statement is appropriate and on the nature of provision to be provided in the statement.

To illustrate this process, let's look at Jane's story.

CASE STUDY

Jane

Jane is now a Year 3 pupil. She was identified and placed on the school SEN register in Year 2. She was provided with School Action. She was identified as having learning difficulties, reflected in her inability to read and spell. She also had poor handwriting and was falling further and further behind. Despite the IEP targets being followed throughout her time in Year 2, Jane failed to make sufficient progress and the school applied for LEA involvement with School Action Plus. As a result, the LEA provided an outside professional to give advice and guidance. However, the gap between Jane and her classmates continued to widen. Her mum was very worried and was willing to support the school with any action it decided to take. It was felt that Jane now needed a statement with the guaranteed TA support that implied.

Jane's school asked the LEA to make a statutory assessment of her needs. Her main problem area was literacy, and this was affecting her ability to cope in subjects like science, geography and history. Numeracy was also affected as Jane was unable to read the questions, even though the actual maths was not a problem. Her behaviour was deteriorating as her self-esteem fell.

Jane needed an individual literacy programme to teach reading, writing and spelling skills. Clearly her teacher, with a class of thirty other pupils, could not provide this. The support of a TA was essential. On a personal level, Jane would also benefit from the relationship she could develop with the TA.

The SENCo provided the LEA with all the necessary SEN paperwork showing what the school had provided for Jane at School Action and School Action Plus. The school had to demonstrate that they had followed the correct procedures and that IEP targets had been established, followed and reviewed regularly. They had to show that, despite all this input, progress was unsatisfactory.

A few weeks later the school and Jane's parents were told that the LEA would carry out a formal statutory assessment. This was completed within twelve weeks. As a result, Jane received a statement to ensure she stayed in her mainstream school. A copy of a draft statement, setting out the provision and conditions of the statement, was sent to the school and to Jane's parents telling them that Jane would receive five hours' TA help each week. Her progress was to be monitored termly by the Learning Support Service, who would offer advice, support and possibly resources.

The parents were given fifteen days to raise objections. None was made, so a copy of the final statement was issued. The TA was employed, the IEP was drawn up and the work could begin.

Statements are reviewed at least annually at meetings which decide upon the provision for the following months. The meetings discuss whether existing provision should continue, whether the hours should stay the same and so on. Very occasionally, but less and less so in these days of inclusion, the LEA may decide the best future for the pupil lies in a special school.

Many factors affect the impact of having a special educational need. These include the severity and complexity of the need itself, home circumstances, the quality of teaching/resources/support in school and, of course, the effectiveness of the TA.

This chapter ends with two moving accounts from TAs which indicate the importance of their role in helping a pupil come to terms with their difficulties.

Sometimes our light goes out, but it is blown into flame by another human being. Each of us owes deepest thanks to those who have re-kindled this light

Albert Schweitzer

Think of a child

Name: __Billy__

Age: __9 years 6 months__

Class: __Year 5__

Name of TA: __Sandra__

Provision: __5 hours per week__

What is the nature of the pupil's special educational need?	Billy has literacy difficulties. His reading and spelling age is three years behind his chronological age and his handwriting is very poor. He forms most of his letters incorrectly. He has low self-esteem and is beginning to be naughty in class. He is also absent from school frequently. When this happens I work with other children who need some help instead.
What is the nature of your involvement with the pupil?	Billy has a statement and the statement provides five hours of TA time each week. I work with him for one hour each day, when the class is having literacy. We stay in the class for the first half-hour of the literacy hour, when I sit next to him and check that he has understood all that the teacher is saying. I also encourage him to put up his hand when he knows the answer. He is so scared of getting it wrong. He does not want the teacher and kids to think he is 'stupid'. He is always saying that he is stupid. I also keep him 'on task' when his attention strays. The other half of the lesson I work with Billy and two other pupils. We are working through a 'second chance' reading scheme which includes resources to help Billy with all his difficulties around reading. Twice a week we do spelling, using the Look Say Cover Write Check method. He is learning to spell the first forty-five high frequency words from the literacy strategy.
How does this special need impact on the life of the pupil?	**At school:** Billy has no confidence. He regards all the other children as clever. He finds it difficult to make friends and complains that he is picked on, but I have noticed that at times he makes such a nuisance of himself with the other children that they lose their tempers and turn on him. It's a shame; he just doesn't know how to make friends. I think he must be very unhappy. He does not like school. **At home:** Billy's mum was willing to work with him at home but he is very reluctant to do anything and she has given up trying. He plays a lot with his little sister, but his behaviour at home is deteriorating and his mum is getting very anxious about him (and I think angry and frustrated with him too).
What I hope to achieve in my role	I hope I can help Billy with his reading and spelling. He will feel a lot better when he begins to make progress. Also I hope to make a good relationship with him as a starting point to helping him relate better to other children. He is already beginning to learn how to make friends in the small group. So we will see. My main hope is that he will want to come to school and will be happy there.
What I need to be careful about	Billy is becoming too dependent on me. He wants to stay in at playtime with me and he hangs around waiting for me. It will not help him in the long run. He needs to learn to stand on his own two feet. I want to build up a close relationship without making it a dependent one.

Think of a child

Name: __Rosie__   Name of TA: __Beryl__

Age: __13 years 3 months__   Provision: __3 hours per week__

Class: __Year 8__

What is the nature of the pupil's special educational need?	A member of the Learning Support Service has assessed Rosie, and she has been told that she has a specific learning difficulty – dyslexia. She has great difficulty with reading and spelling, and she also has low self-esteem. Her problems were late in being recognised because when she was in the primary school she moved from school to school through changing home circumstances and was never properly assessed. She seems more settled now, and has been in this school for over a year.
What is the nature of your involvement with the pupil?	Rosie has just been assessed at School Action Plus and the LEA have given her three hours of my support for a period of six months after which this will be reviewed to see how she is progressing. She has an IEP that the SENCo and the specialist teacher devised between them. I go into school for one hour on Monday, Wednesday and Friday. It is easy for me as my son goes to this school so I take him and go straight into the school. I work with her out of the class, in a room on our own. We have been working together for two weeks and Rosie says she enjoys these sessions with me and is happy to leave the class.
How does this special need impact on the life of the pupil?	**At school:** Rosie is quiet and withdrawn. She has one friend but they fall out from time to time and then she gets very upset. She finds it hard to make other friends. Although she is very bright and can talk about anything, in the class she is very quiet and, I think, ashamed of her inability to read and write. She likes coming out of the class as no one can see the level of work she is doing. She is falling behind in other lessons. Although she understands the work, she often cannot read the questions and does not like to say so as she feels ashamed. Her work is sometimes poor. **At home:** Rosie has two sisters who are younger than she is and they both can read and spell better than she can. This does not help her self-esteem and her mother tells me she is often very bossy towards her sisters. I cannot imagine that as she is so quiet at school. I think she is unhappy and that disturbs me.
What I hope to achieve in my role	I want Rosie to get better at spelling so she can do the work in class. I think she has dropped so far behind the others that she needs more TA time so that I can help her in other lessons. However, Rosie says she does not want this as she will feel stupid having me next to her. I feel worried about her and will discuss what needs to be done with the SENCo at our weekly meeting.

How to
cope

Chapter 3
How to cope with children with special needs

What exactly do we mean by special educational needs? The 2002 edition of the Code of Practice describes special needs in this way:

A child has special educational needs if they have a learning difficulty, which calls for special educational provision to be made for them.

A child has a learning difficulty if they:
a)   have a significantly greater difficulty in learning than the majority of children of the same age; or
b)   have a disability which prevents or hinders them from making use of educational facilities of a kind generally provided for children of the same age in schools within the area of the local education authority;
c)   is under compulsory school age and falls within the definition of a) or b) above or would do so if special educational provision were not made for them.

A child must not be regarded as having a learning difficulty solely because the language or form of language of their home is different from the language in which they are taught

Special educational provision means:
a)   for a child of 2 years old or over, educational provision which is additional to or otherwise different from the educational provision made generally for children of their age in schools maintained by the LEA, other than special schools in the area;
b)   for a child under 2, educational provision of any kind.

(Education Act 1996, section 312)

The 2002 Code identifies four main areas of SEN:
1)   Cognition and learning difficulties
2)   Emotional, behavioural and social difficulties
3)   Communication and interaction difficulties
4)   Sensory and/or physical difficulties.

A pupil may have problems in more than one area. For example, a child may have a learning difficulty and a behavioural one.
        Let us look at the four areas in more detail, as identified in the SEN Thresholds' Good Practice Guidance (draft SEN Code of Practice, July 2000).

Cognition and learning difficulties

There are two main areas here, general learning difficulties and specific learning difficulties.

General learning difficulties

These pupils are likely to show:

- low levels of attainment in all forms of assessment including, for younger children, baseline assessments;
- difficulty in acquiring skills (noticeably in literacy and numeracy) on which much other learning in school depends;
- difficulty in dealing with abstract ideas and generalising from experience;
- a range of associated difficulties, notably in speech and language (particularly for younger children) and in social and emotional development.

CASE STUDY

Usma works with Joe, a pupil with a statement, for three hours a week. He has been assessed as having general learning difficulties. Usma's time is mainly divided into supporting Joe in class during the literacy and numeracy sessions when she supports Joe by working towards the targets on his IEP. For one half-hour session a week, Usma works in a 1:1 situation with Joe, and for another half-hour she works with him in a small group of pupils experiencing similar difficulties. The work carried out in the group focuses on the development of phonics/spelling/writing skills, using a variety of resources from within the school. The educational psychologist is also involved with Joe and visits him every month to assess his progress and offer advice and support to the school. The programme of work carried out by Usma is reflected in the teacher's planning.

Specific learning difficulties

Some pupils will experience difficulties with learning in certain specific areas. These pupils may be found to have dyslexia or dyspraxia. They are likely to have problems in one or more of the following areas:

- difficulties with fine or gross motor skills;
- low attainment in one or more curriculum areas, particularly when this can be traced to difficulties in some aspects of underlying literacy and/or numeracy skills;
- inconsistency in attainment (e.g. better oral than written work);
- signs of frustration and/or low self-esteem, taking the form, in some cases, of behavioural difficulties;

- difficulties with tasks involving specific skills such as sequencing and organisation or phonological or short-term memory abilities;
- in younger children, language difficulties such as limited skills in verbal exchanges or in following instructions; evident difficulties or delays in forming concepts, especially when information requires first-hand sensory experiences.

CASE STUDY

Karen works with Hannah who has been assessed as having dyslexia. Hannah is a very bright and articulate pupil but she experiences great problems with reading and spelling, which are leading to a sense of frustration and a deterioration in her behaviour. The advice on her IEP came from a specialist visiting teacher, who has also trained Karen to deliver the programme of work devised to support Hannah. Hannah has been given support at School Action Plus and does not have a statement. Karen works with Hannah for two hours per week in a 1:1 situation delivering the programme. She meets with the SENCo once a week, when she is able to discuss Hannah's progress.

Emotional, behavioural and social difficulties

Pupils experiencing these difficulties are likely to show:

- age-inappropriate behaviour or behaviour that seems otherwise socially inappropriate or strange;
- behaviour that interferes with the learning of the pupil or their peers (e.g. persistent calling out in class, refusal to work, persistent annoyance of peers);
- signs of emotional turbulence (e.g. unusual tearfulness, withdrawal from social situations);
- difficulties in forming and maintaining positive relationships (e.g. isolation from peers, aggressiveness to peers and adults).

CASE STUDY

Pat supports Della who has emotional and behavioural difficulties. Della has a statement giving her seven hours of provision a week, five hours of which are provided within the classroom, where Pat ensures Della stays on task. Pat spends one hour 1:1 with Della working on targets set in the IEP. The remaining hour is spent in a small group to help Della build relationship skills. Pat works on Della's low self-esteem throughout.

Communication and interaction difficulties

These pupils will fit into two main areas, those who experience speech and language difficulties and those with autistic spectrum disorders.

Speech and language difficulties

Pupils in this category are likely to have difficulty in the following areas:

- ⊙ the production of speech;
- ⊙ finding words and joining them together in meaningful and expressive language;
- ⊙ communicating through speech and other forms of language;
- ⊙ understanding or responding to the verbal cues of others;
- ⊙ the acquisition and expression of thoughts and ideas;
- ⊙ understanding and using appropriate social language;
- ⊙ frustration and anxieties arising from a failure to communicate, possibly leading to apparent behavioural difficulties and deteriorating social and peer relationships.

CASE STUDY

Jamie has been provided with School Action Plus because he has severe speech problems and it is very difficult for anyone to understand what he is saying. He has the support of Adrian for three hours a week. Adrian has received specific training and guidance from a speech and language therapist, who visits him every six weeks to discuss the effectiveness of the programme with him, the class teacher and the SENCo. The IEP indicates very clear guidelines, teaching strategies and resources. Adrian's particular role is to deliver a language development programme devised by the speech therapist. This is delivered in a 1:1 situation as Jamie's needs are very specific and no other child would benefit from working on this particular programme.

Autistic spectrum disorders

Pupils with this disorder may have difficulties with social relationships, social communication and imaginative thought. They may show:

- ⊙ difficulties in attuning to social situations and responding to normal environmental cues;
- ⊙ evidence of emerging personal agendas that are increasingly not amenable to adult direction;
- ⊙ a tendency to withdraw from social situations and an increasing passivity and absence of initiative;
- ⊙ repressed, reduced or inappropriate social interactions extending to

highly egocentric behaviour with an absence of awareness of the needs and emotions of others;

⊙ impaired use of language, either expressive or receptive – this may include odd intonation, forms and limited expression, reducing the potential for two-way communication;

⊙ limitations in expressive or creative peer activities, extending to obsessive interests or repetitive activities.

CASE STUDY

Alice works with Sadie for ten hours a week. Sadie is autistic and has a statement. IEP targets are concerned with Sadie's emotional and learning difficulties, and are aimed at developing social skills. Most work takes place in a small group as Sadie finds it difficult to cope in the classroom situation. By encouraging Sadie to interact with others in the group and by giving her the chance to see how other children relate to one another, it is hoped to help Sadie with her ability to relate to other children. When Alice is not timetabled to work with Sadie she works with the rest of the class.

Sensory and physical difficulties

These difficulties include pupils who may have:

⊙ hearing impairment;
⊙ visual impairment;
⊙ physical and medical difficulties.

Hearing impairment

These pupils' problems will range from mild to severe and show up in the following ways:

⊙ deterioration in academic performance, such as handwriting, speech, lack of response to verbal cues or increasing requests for repetition of instructions;

⊙ physical changes such as persistent discharge from the ears, tilting of the head to hear better, or a need to focus on the teacher's face when instructions are being given;

⊙ increased reliance on classmates to relay or clarify instructions;

⊙ frustration with themselves or with others for no apparent reason, leading to emotional or behavioural problems.

CASE STUDY

Sally works with Parvinder, who has a statement, for five hours a week. He has significant hearing loss and wears a hearing aid. Parvinder has learning difficulties and problems in forming relationships with other children. Sally follows IEP targets and regularly meets with the Hearing Impaired Service. She also works on Parvinder's low self-esteem to help him build relationships with his peers. Some support is on a 1:1 basis and for three hours a week he works in a small group.

Visual impairment

The indicators for this category are:

- ⊙ possible deterioration in handwriting, slowness in copying from the board, asking for written instructions to be given verbally;
- ⊙ deterioration in hand-eye coordination, excessive straining of the eyes to read the board, needing to be at the front of the class to see the TV, pictures in books etc.;
- ⊙ anxiety in performing certain physical activities in PE or in moving around the playground;
- ⊙ evidence of stress leading to withdrawn or frustrated behaviour.

CASE STUDY

Lucy works with Pete who has a statement owing to deteriorating sight. This has led to limited progress in learning tasks and a consequent loss of confidence. Normal-print-size books are difficult for Pete to read. His IEP includes the use of low-vision aids like a raised desk top and a special magnifying glass. Lucy also makes enlarged photocopies of worksheets for him. She meets regularly with a member of the Vision Impaired Service, who monitors Pete's progress, to discuss Pete's provision and progress.

Physical and medical difficulties

Only pupils whose medical or physical conditions prevent them from access to the curriculum, thereby creating a special educational need, should be included here. Conditions to look out for include:

- ⊙ evidence of a learning difficulty;
- ⊙ disability that affects the pupil's confidence, self-esteem, emotional stability or relationship with peers;
- ⊙ disability that impacts on classroom performance because of lack of concentration, drowsiness or lack of motivation;
- ⊙ disability that impacts on other areas of the curriculum, e.g. PE.

CASE STUDY

Jane works with Sharon for two hours a week. Sharon's needs are met through School Action Plus. Sharon lost the use of her right hand in an accident. Her school developed a programme in consultation with an occupational therapist, who also advised on the use of equipment designed for left-handed people. Sharon has made such good progress that the ten hours originally allocated to her have been cut to two. Jane still works in the school for ten hours a week, now spending eight hours with other SEN pupils.

This chapter has shown how varied, interesting and challenging the work of a TA is. You will almost certainly be working with pupils who fit into one or more of the areas outlined, unless you are specifically employed to work as a general support.

How to
get
the
job

Chapter 4
How to get the job

Here are three accounts of how people became TAs.

My name is Kerry. My friend was a teacher at the school and when a child in her class received a statement and they were looking for someone for ten hours a week she told me about it. I rang up the school and they sent me an application form. The job was advertised in the local paper as well and I had to be interviewed. There were three other people there but I got the job. I have been so grateful to my friend ever since. I love my job, but I don't think I would have had the courage to apply for it without her support and encouragement.

My name is Elizabeth and I now work for fifteen hours a week in a special needs unit for pupils with hearing difficulties. It is attached to a mainstream school and the pupils spend some of their time in the unit and some in the school. This is how I got my job, which I have been doing for ten years. Twelve years ago, when my son was still at junior school, I started to work there voluntarily for three mornings a week, mostly hearing children read. I enjoyed it very much. One day I was reading through the job sheets in the staff room and saw my present job advertised. I rang the school, filled in the application form and went for the interview. I hadn't done any paid work for ten years but I think my experience working voluntarily in my son's school helped and I got the job.

I am Pat and I am working in school with a pupil with a statement. I also teach the Additional Literacy Support programme, for which I underwent training provided by the LEA. Eight years ago I saw the job advertised in the local paper. At that time it was to support a different pupil who had a statement for five hours a week. My own children were all at school and I had helped out voluntarily there hearing pupils read, helping small groups of pupils with cooking and occasionally going with teachers on school trips and visits. I used to be on the PTA committee as well and helped to organise fund-raising events. I wanted to have a job that fitted in with them so this seemed ideal. I rang the school, filled in the application form, had the interview, got the job and never looked back.

Usually schools start the search for a TA by placing an ad in the local newspaper. Schools often get an enormous response. One head teacher recently advertised for a SENCo and had no response, in the same week getting 163 responses for a TA post. If you are thinking about applying, consider the following:

- Is this a job which interests me?
- Can I work the times required by the school?
- Can I make the necessary arrangements to accommodate the needs of my own children to enable me to get to school on time?
- Will I be able to reach the school easily?
- Does the advertisement ask for any qualifications and, if so, do I have them or something equivalent?
- Is the pay adequate for my needs?
- Will I fit in?
- Will I be able to cope with the demands of the job?

It is natural that you will be anxious about applying for a job, particularly if you have been out of work for some time bringing up your own children. But everyone will be feeling much the same, so just feel the fear and do it anyway.

Be prepared

Questions you may want to ask at your interview:

- What exactly will my role be?
- Will I have any training before I start?
- What training opportunities are available?
- What will my hours be?
- What is the pay?
- Will I get holiday/sick pay?
- Will my contract be temporary/permanent?

What the school is looking for

The major factors are:

- Some kind of qualification.
- Ability to work as part of a team.
- Previous experience with children.
- Skills you can bring to the job.
- Ability to get on with adults as well as children.
- Initiative.
- Previous work record.

Some of the questions you may be asked

- What qualities do you think a good TA would need to have and do you have them?
- What has your previous work experience been?
- Do you have any qualifications?
- What would you do if you were asked to create a display?
- Would you be willing to volunteer to support the occasional out-of-hours school function?
- Are you computer literate?
- What would you do if a child in one of your groups was refusing to work?
- What are your hobbies/interests?

Here are some examples of how not to respond to interview questions:

- *Why did you apply for this job?*
  'Because I am fed up with being at home/Because my husband made me/Because my children come to the school and I want to keep my eye on them/I don't know.'
- *What is your previous experience with children?*
  'Well, I was a child myself once.'
- *What skills could you bring to the job?* (e.g. painting, clay modelling, sign language, first-aid skills and experience, playing an instrument)
  'None. I was never good at anything.'

The interview

You will be given a specific time and date for interview. When you arrive you will almost certainly find yourself waiting with the other short-listed candidates. It is unlikely that more than three or four candidates will be selected for interview, so remember that you have all done well to get this far. Many other applicants will not have been offered an interview.

Interview panels vary but will almost certainly include the head and a governor of the school. The SENCo may also attend. At this stage, don't worry if you lack qualifications or training. They are looking at the whole person and they may choose you even if you have no qualifications and others have. Alternatively they may prefer someone with more experience with children than you. It all depends on the school's priorities at the time.

Just be yourself and answer the questions to the best of your ability.

FOOD FOR THOUGHT

You can change your mind

As they are interviewing you, you must interview them. Ask yourself if you would feel happy working in school with the people interviewing you. If you don't think you would, you can always say you don't think it's the right job for you after all. That is better than starting the job and giving up after a few weeks.

Not this time

If at first you don't succeed, try, try again.

If you fail at first don't be disillusioned. TA jobs come up all the time. The government is investing lots of money to raise standards and deal effectively with pupils with SEN, and TAs play a big part in this. After the interview it might be useful to reflect on why another person got the job. Maybe it would help to work voluntarily in school to gain experience. Perhaps you could study for some kind of qualification. Also, bear in mind that if they liked you the head will have your details and is likely to contact you if another job appears.

Success

Congratulations! A new phase in your life is about to begin with opportunities to develop your knowledge and skills, to meet people from many different walks of life and to make a real difference in the lives of vulnerable children.

Anyone who works with children has to have a police check. The LEA will organise this when the school informs them of your appointment. You will be able to begin your job immediately but if the police check reveals any problem you may not be allowed to continue. Assuming all is well, you will be issued with your contract, be it temporary or permanent, and a job description that outlines exactly what your duties are. If you are happy with that, you are ready to begin your new life officially.

The longer I live the more I am convinced that the one thing worth living for is the privilege of making someone else happy.

Booker T Washington

Chapter 5
What does the job involve?

You may be involved in some or all of the following:

- Supporting pupils within the whole class.
- Working with groups.
- Working with individual pupils.

Below we look at each of these in detail.

HANDY HINTS

Before you start be prepared. Have a box of tricks ready with all the equipment you may need, like:

- Pupils' books.
- Resources. (A word of warning: don't hog all the teaching materials. They should be stored centrally and used only when you need them. Prior to every lesson get the resources you need and always replace them when you have finished.)
- Pencils, pencil sharpeners and rubbers. (Make sure that what you give out you get back. Equipment has a habit of mysteriously disappearing. The same applies to games you play. Ensure every last card is collected since missing items render games meaningless; then pupils get bored, which can lead to behavioural problems.)
- Stickers/certificates or whatever the school uses to reward the pupils.

Supporting pupils within the whole class

Teachers may involve TAs in the following tasks:

- Adapting materials to support pupils in different areas of the curriculum.
- Preparing equipment for cooking, science, art, etc.
- Accompanying children, with teachers, on school trips/visits.
- Looking after the library.
- Making resources and worksheets.

- First aid.
- Working with pupils on computers.
- Accompanying children who are accommodated in special units to classes in mainstream schools.
- Attending swimming sessions with teacher and children.
- Attending review meetings.
- Attending literacy/numeracy planning sessions.
- Supporting pupils in literacy and numeracy lessons.

It is likely that you will be involved in the support of pupils in these sessions if you work in a primary school. The DfEE's TA File, issued in September 2000 to be used as initial training for TAs, offers some good ideas for supporting pupils in the Literacy Hour. The key ones are listed below.

- *Drawing in reticent pupils – these pupils are too timid to put their hands up.*
  'Sally has a good idea. Tell them, Sally.'
- *Getting the ball rolling when pupils are slow to start a discussion.*
  'Lucy, tell everyone about the animal we saw the other day in the zoo book and the sort of food he liked to eat.'
- *Supportive behaviour for less able or less confident pupils.*
  These pupils need unobtrusive nodding, smiling, winking and eye contact.
- *Joining in.*
  Joining in yourself and making your own contributions to class discussions.
- *Demonstrating for the teacher.*
  Telling the teacher how you worked out a spelling, how you found a word in the dictionary, or explaining some other way in which you found an answer to the teacher's question.
- *Acting as devil's advocate.*
  Asking the teacher to explain something more fully (on behalf of a pupil whom you think might need more information about a particular point).
- *Echoing the teacher by repeating or rewording the phrase for pupils who may need help.*
  'Look, Hannah, Mr Stokes is showing you where the speech marks are. We know about those, don't we?'
- *Acting as an extra pair of eyes.*
  Observing the pupils and noticing which pupils clearly do not understand, which pupils are not listening and at which particular point in the lesson the problem arose.
- *Assisting with behaviour management.*
  You can sit by a pupil who finds it hard to stay on task and is likely to be disruptive. At times you may need to take them out of the class and carry on working with them elsewhere, which is another

reason why it is important that you are involved with the class planning.

- ⊙ *Resource management.*
  This will include preparing, distributing and collecting pupil resources, and helping pupils use the resources.

You may be asked to support the class in areas of the curriculum other than literacy. This is common practice in secondary schools and may involve preparation for lessons like geography, history, science and ICT. If you are supporting a pupil with severe and complex needs across the curriculum, you may be involved in:

- ⊙ preparing resources;
- ⊙ accompanying the child to the toilet;
- ⊙ supervising the child in the playground at lunchtime;
- ⊙ checking equipment (e.g. hearing aids, wheel-chairs);
- ⊙ carrying out exercise programmes under supervision.

Working with groups

The teacher will select the pupils with whom you work. They may be a group of low-ability pupils; your job will be to offer support or to consolidate work from a previous literacy or numeracy lesson. You may support a group of high achievers. It all depends on your job description and why you have been employed in the first place.

In some cases, children will have been chosen to work alongside the statemented pupil you are responsible for. The stimulation of group work is important, but if you find the group selected is distracting you from meeting the needs of your pupil discuss this with the teacher. Also, ensure the group is working around the same level as your pupil. If there are behavioural problems in the group, say so. Behaviour management training might be helpful. Do not suffer in silence. Class teachers can only offer support if you tell them problems exist.

Working with individual pupils

This form of support is appropriate if a pupil has an IEP with learning goals specific to their needs, and when there is no benefit in involving other pupils. For example, this might be the case with a pupil with severe language difficulties who has a programme devised by a speech and language therapist, or with a dyspraxic pupil who has a daily exercise programme.

When working with a pupil with a statement you are funded by the LEA. If the pupil makes progress to the extent that they no longer need a statement or your support, your support will be withdrawn and you may be out of a job. Don't worry if that happens. You will have gained valuable experience and will find yourself much in demand. The fact that one particular pupil and school no longer need you is a matter of celebration. It's a bit like when your own children grow up and leave home – a time for celebration and sadness.

Your role with an individual pupil may involve offering support across the curriculum. For example, a pupil with physical problems may need help in PE, while a pupil with severe vision impairment may need your full-time support in every lesson. In secondary schools it is usual for the TA to provide this kind of support. This is why it is important to be aware of the focus of the lesson beforehand so you can be adequately prepared. Supplying your pupil with appropriate word banks is often useful.

Whatever the situation, you should receive support and guidance from the class teacher, the SENCo and possibly an outside professional. They should all advise you on targets to work towards and resources and teaching strategies to use.

Whether working within the class, in groups or on an individual basis, there are a number of skills you should seek to develop:

- motivating pupils to work;
- understanding and dealing with difficult behaviour;
- encouraging independence;
- encouraging the growth of pupils' self-esteem.

Children need encouragement, praise and rewards to motivate them to succeed. This is particularly the case with pupils with learning difficulties since many become disillusioned and reluctant to work. They may feel embarrassed about the quality of their work in comparison to that of their classmates.

Praising pupils is a good way of helping them feel good about themselves. It doesn't always work since some pupils with low self-esteem will doubt your sincerity. Other techniques are required in these cases, and we shall discuss these shortly. For children who do respond to praise, here are some ideas.

Ways of offering praise and rewards

Most pupils love to receive stickers – but not all. You would not give Gav in Year 8, with his shaven head and big boots, a sticker with a teddy bear on it saying 'Well done'. He would appreciate a type of reward that relates to his preferences. If he enjoys the computer then reward him with five minutes on it before break. Base the reward on your knowledge of the child.

You will need to know what the general reward system of the school is. House points, certificates or other acknowledgements need to be incorporated into your own reward system. Verbal praise is good too. A 'Well done, Gav' at the right moment, or even a smile or nod of the head, helps to get your message over and keep Gav on task for an increased period of time.

Children enjoy the most bizarre rewards. Being allowed to do any sort of job – from giving out the registers, showing a visitor to the head teacher's office,

Let's remember that our children's spirits are more important than any material things. When we do self-esteem and love blossom and grow more beautifully than any bed of flowers ever would

Jack Canfield

giving the books out to scrubbing the paint pots — has been received with delight during my own time in schools. Children might regard being given menial tasks as rewards for all sorts of reasons, but the key one is that it shows you trust them to do something responsible. It bestows on them a sense of importance.

Praising quietly

Your praise and reward system has to be more subtle for many children with low self-esteem. Place more emphasis on the use of body language. A touch on the shoulder, a wink or a thumbs up to show you've noticed the quality or effort put into their work can work wonders. Show them you are on their side. Stick up for them if someone is unfair or unkind; ask how they enjoyed the football match they watched last night; smile at them when you pass them in the corridor. Acknowledge their presence without making it too big a deal. As your

Keep a low profile

relationship with them grows and their self-esteem develops you can move on to use the same kind of praise and reward system you use with other pupils. Your self-esteem will grow at the same time when you see that your unobtrusive intervention has been effective.

Encouraging the growth of pupils' self-esteem

Self-esteem is about the value a person gives to their own worth. People with high self-esteem place a great value on themselves, believing they are worthwhile people. They are often creative and successful, capable of making healthy and lasting relationships. On the other hand, people who have low self-esteem do not value themselves and feel unworthy. They will treat themselves and others badly (though this will largely be out of their conscious control). They are more likely to be involved in crime, prostitution, drug and alcohol abuse, and may develop mental illness or be involved in unsatisfying relationships.

*I can because
I think I can*

The TA is in a powerful position to offer support in this area since your situation often involves opportunities to build closer relationships with children than the teacher has. You often work in 1:1 situations and in small groups. Through the quality of the relationship you build, the struggling pupil's self-esteem can develop.

How do we know if a pupil has low self-esteem?

The following list is taken from *Windows to our Children* by Violet Oaklander, published by Real People Press.

Some common signs of low self-esteem are:

- ⊙ whining;

- needing to win;
- cheating in games;
- needing to be perfect;
- exaggerated bragging;
- giving away money, sweets, toys etc.;
- attention seeking, fooling around and clowning;
- teasing others;
- anti-social behaviour;
- being self-critical, withdrawn or shy;
- blaming others for everything;
- making excuses for everything;
- constantly apologising;
- fear of trying new things;
- distrusting people;
- wanting many new things;
- behaving defensively;
- over-eating;
- over-pleasing;
- inability to make choices and decisions;
- never saying 'no';
- never saying 'yes'.

There are no words to express the abyss between isolation and having an ally. It may be conceded to the mathematician that four is twice two. But two is not twice one; two is two thousand times one.

G K Chesterton

Many pupils with SEN have low self-esteem. They know, through comparing their work with that of others, that their skills are less well developed. They will often identify themselves as being 'thick'. Fellow-pupils sometimes use such a word to describe them. Forbid the word in your presence. Make it clear that you want everyone to do their best, not spend their time criticising the work or appearance of others. Pupils with SEN are often very vulnerable and need support in standing up to bullying.

Dennis Lawrence, author of *Enhancing Self-esteem in the Classroom (1996),* says:

> *A vast body of evidence has accumulated showing a positive correlation between self-esteem and achievement, and with regard to self-esteem and school achievement in particular ... There is clear evidence that relationships between teachers [and that includes TAs] and students can be either conducive to the enhancement of high self-esteem or conducive towards reducing self-esteem.*

FOOD FOR THOUGHT

Ideas for raising a child's self-esteem

1) Show the child you care about them.
   'You have tried so hard today. I'm really proud of you.'

2) Be on time for your lesson or group/individual session. If you are not going to be there, explain why to the children the previous day.
   'I'll miss you all tomorrow, and I want to say I'm sorry that I won't be able to be here. I am going off on a training course which is important to me, but I will see you as usual on the next day.'

3) Have all your equipment ready and make sure the room you are working is as comfortable as you can make it.

4) Make an effort to remember all the children's names and birthdays.
   'I have written your names on these sticky labels. Would you mind wearing them until I learn your names?'

5) Say 'Sorry' if you make a mistake.

6) Make sure that the work you are doing is appropriate for the pupil – not too easy or too difficult. If you feel there is a problem discuss this with the teacher.

7) Thank children for any job they have done or contribution they may have made during the session.

8) Do not allow pupils to abuse you or each other and never criticise the pupil, only the negative behaviour.
   'Paul, I will not allow you to speak to other children in this group in that way. Sally now feels upset as you called her a name. What can you do to put it right?'

9) Treat pupils equally and with respect at all times.

10) Listen to what pupils want to tell you, without allowing this to impinge too much on the lesson.
    'Helen, I really want to hear about the dance competition, but could you tell me about it at the end of the lesson?' (It's amazing how the desire to tell you a long and detailed story in lesson time disappears when playtime comes.)

11) Remember to ask how a child's sick grandma is or how their dog got on at the vet's after his operation. If a child goes into hospital, send a card.

12) When the child leaves the session with you, say goodbye and tell them that you look forward to the next session.

13) Watch out for any sign of child abuse and report this immediately to the class or head teacher.

I expect you will be able to add many more ideas to this list.

Understand and deal with difficult behaviour

Learn the school rules and, in particular, the systems for praising and rewarding the pupils. Pupils can be very canny, and may try to trick you into imparting house points. They may say, 'Oh, Miss always gives us a house-point every time we finish a piece of work.' This is unlikely, but check all the same. Use the set of rules the pupils are used to and do not be taken in.

Find out what the school approach to discipline is and what sanctions are available. Have an arrangement with the class teacher about what to do if a pupil in your group misbehaves. You should be able to send that pupil back to the class if the situation becomes intolerable, and discuss the matter with the teacher after the lesson. It may be that this pupil is too difficult for you to handle and should be removed from the group or it may just have been an isolated incident. No matter what, always wipe the slate clean. Never bear a grudge.

Always carry out your promises, including your sanctions. If you say a pupil's behaviour is unsatisfactory and that you are going to discuss it with the teacher, do so. If you don't keep your word, children will lose respect for you, which could result in behavioural problems.

FOOD FOR THOUGHT

Encouraging independence

You work with Sean, a statemented pupil, for ten hours a week. You see him struggle with his work. You know a bit about the family background and are aware that things are difficult. You get to know him and want to help him all you can. The skill is to do this whilst encouraging his self-reliance.

Worst-case scenario

Sean feels secure with you. You are a kind and compassionate person, which is why you got the job in the first place. He wants to be with you all the time. You are pleased that someone should need you so much. You encourage Sean's increasing attachment. You allow him to stay in at playtimes with you and give him little jobs to do as you know he does not like going out to play. You bring him your own children's old toys and sometimes even their discarded clothes. You help him with his work to the extent that you are more responsible for the work he produces than he is. His dependency grows.

Then one day he announces that the family is to move. And what has he learned from you? That he is incapable of working independently and that without you he is unable to produce stories. He is unable to spell or do his maths independently as he has always had you to help. He has no idea how to deal with playground bullies or how to make friends as he has always had you. His prospects in the next school are grim. Your qualities of kindness and compassion have been misused.

Best-case scenario

Sean feels secure with you. You encourage the relationship, letting him know that you value and accept him just as he is. You will not allow other pupils to bully him and will deal with this if and when it occurs. But you have high expectations of him. You will not accept work from him into which he has put little effort. You will teach him how to become an independent speller, either by showing him how to use the dictionary or by providing a list of words he may encounter. He should have a wordbook in which to write down the words he finds difficult. You will discuss his writing with him and provide a framework to help him produce well-sequenced and correctly constructed stories. You will discuss with him the strengths and weaknesses of his work and help the teacher and SENCo to produce appropriate targets on his

IEP. You will help him understand basic mathematical concepts and encourage him to have a go.

When he is reluctant to go into the playground, you will find out why and discuss with him strategies for dealing with whatever he finds difficult. You may encourage other pupils to play with him in the playground. You will check to see if he is OK and if not will involve the teacher or SENCo. You will understand that enabling Sean to deal with difficult situations is far more important than rescuing him from them. When he moves on, he will be an independent, confident boy.

To know someone here or there,
with whom you feel there is
an understanding in spite of
distances or thoughts unexpressed –
that can make of this earth a garden

Goethe

Chapter 6
Supporting literacy –
hearing readers

The TA will inevitably support pupils with literacy and numeracy, which will involve hearing pupils read. This may mean working with specific pupils with difficulties or more generally hearing all pupils read. You will always work under the direction of the teacher or SENCo.

Before you start

Make sure the book you are using is at an appropriate level. Younger readers will be reading books that challenge them and there will be words that they do not understand. If children are unable to read more than two words in every ten, they will need a different book to prevent frustration and a sense of failure.

Less able readers and younger readers need to be taught reading strategies. There are four main ones:

- Use of picture cues
- Use of sight vocabulary
- Use of context cues
- Use of phonics.

Picture cues

The first strategy we all used when learning to read was using cues from the pictures. For example, we were able to recognise the round red thing in the book as a ball. When we saw a picture of a ball with the word 'ball' underneath, we began to get the idea that the object was also represented by a word. With struggling or early readers the information offered by the picture is important. If there is a picture on the page, discuss it with the child before they read the text and make sure they verbalise the words from the picture.

Discussing the picture helps children gain an understanding of what the text is about. It is a useful aid to building up the pupil's spoken vocabulary.

Never assume pupils know the names of things. I have worked with 8-year-olds who did not know a cow from a sheep, and 13-year-olds who could not give a name to zebras or giraffes. This poor vocabulary may be a reflection of home circumstances in which there is little conversation or looking at books and few or no stimulating trips out; or it may indicate a difficulty the pupil has with making sense of language. Either way, it is important that vocabulary is discussed.

Sight vocabulary

Before pupils get their first reading book they will usually have acquired a small 'sight vocabulary' (words they can read). The growth of a 'spoken vocabulary' and the development of a basic knowledge of language precede this.

Gradually, from around the age of 18 months, children recognise and name various objects – Mummy, Dad, Nan, pen, book and so on. Around the age of 3 to 4 years, many children begin to recognise words as well as objects, and so begin to read. Children begin to acquire a sight vocabulary of words from their reading books, ('Look Mummy, that says cat!'), the television or computer and through visits to shops. The first word one child I know was able to read was 'Sainsbury's'!

Often the first word recognised and read is their own name. In nursery and reception classes you will see teachers labelling objects in the room: door, wall, floor and so on to encourage reading.

The words which pupils are taught in school are dictated by the National Literacy Strategy and are printed below. These words are known as the high frequency words since they form about 75 per cent of all the words we read and write. In addition to these words pupils will also need to learn the key words from whatever reading scheme is used in the school. For example, Oxford Reading Tree schools would teach the words Floppy, Kipper and so on; while Ginn readers would need to learn Ben and Ladd. These words differ according to the scheme.

The high frequency words, which are grouped here by frequency and difficulty, are words which are meant to be taught to pupils in Key Stage 1. If you are working with pupils with SEN in Key Stages 2 and 3, you may need to teach some of these words still.

Reception words (45)

I	and	he	is	a	to	the	in	was	of
it	we	on	at	for	said	you	are	they	all
up	look	like	go	this	come	big	my	no	get
went	me	she	see	can	going	away	play	am	cat
day	dog	mum	dad	yes					

Years 1 and 2 words

as	be	but	had	have	him	his	not	one	so
with	little	down	old	new	that	then	want	when	where
will	an	over	make	has	or	if	did	two	came
back	been	by	call	called	can't	could	do	first	from
her	her	just	made	more	much	now	off	our	out
some	their	them	there	were	what	your	ball	bed	jump
got	than	man	ran	good	girl	us	dig	house	about
again	another	because	brother	don't	door	half	help	home	how
last	laugh	live	lived	love	many	may	name	next	night
once	people	push	pull	put	saw	school	seen	should	sister
take	these	three	time	too	took	tree	very	water	way
would									

In addition Key Stage 1 pupils are meant to be able to read:

> days of the week;
> months of the year;
> numbers to twenty;
> common colour words;
> pupils' name and address;
> name and address of school.

Medium frequency words to be taught in Year 4

ask	asked	began	being	brought	can't	change	coming	didn't	does
don't	found	goes	gone	heard	I'm	jumped	knew	know	leave
might	opened	show	started	think	thought	told	tries	turn	turned
used	walk	walked	walking	watch	write	woke	woken	almost	always
any	before	better	during	every	first	half	morning	much	ever
number	often	only	second	sometimes	still	suddenly	today	until	upon
while	year	young	above	across	along	also	around	below	between
both	different	following	high	inside	near	other	outside	place	right
round	such	through	together	under	where	without			

Medium frequency words to be taught in Year 5

baby	balloon	birthday	brother	children	clothes	garden	great	happy	head
something	sure	swimming	those	word	work	world	earth	eyes	father
friends	important	lady	light	money	mother	own	paper	sister	small
sound	white	why	window						

Don't worry about which words to teach or how to go about that. All of this information should be included in the pupil's IEP. (Have a look at the sample IEP on page 51 to give you some idea of what to expect.) Any training you will need to support the pupils is the responsibility of the SENCo or the teacher. The school may decide to send you on training courses run by the LEA or another training provider.

Context cues

Pupils bring their knowledge of the world to reading.

Take the example of Suzie Brighteyes, aged 5, who has been round the world twice, is taken out every weekend on stimulating visits and whose parents read to her every night. She lives in a secure and loving environment with parents who explain everything and value and ask for her opinion. Consequently, not only does she bring her extensive vocabulary and understanding to reading, she also brings confidence.

If Suzie Brighteyes meets the sentence, 'The boy went to the museum and saw a d...', she would be able to guess the word 'dinosaur'. She's been to a museum, seen a dinosaur skeleton and would be confident enough to try her luck. Because she can understand what she is reading she can self-correct. She will also be able to predict what may happen next in the story.

Jimmy, however, has seldom been past the end of his street, is part of a huge and dysfunctional family, has never seen the sea or been near a zoo or a museum and lives in a house with no books in which he is rarely spoken to. He will bring that experience to reading.

He probably won't know what a museum is, much less a dinosaur, so he would not be able to use the meaning of the text to acquire the word. He is quite likely to say something like 'The boy went to the museum and saw a deep.' He has a lack of understanding of the text so he is not able to use context cues to support his reading.

This is where the picture, if there is one, can come in handy. Jimmy needs to be shown a picture so he can see what a dinosaur looks like and be told just what a museum is in order to build up his limited knowledge and understanding of the world. You can see the value of well-chosen school trips for boys and girls with Jimmy's lack of experience. There is nothing like exposing children to reality to engage their attention and help them to learn.

Jimmy's self-esteem will suffer when he sees Suzie succeeding where he fails. We may understand why he fails, but he won't. He will just perceive himself to be inferior.

Jimmy's incorrect use of grammar may also put him at a disadvantage. If he is used to saying, for example, 'They was naughty children', he will struggle when he attempts to read grammatically correct sentences in his school book. It's difficult for pupils who come to school when their life has not prepared them for the world of reading. It is part of the TA's job to try and make up for this deficit.

Phonics

When pupils encounter words which are not in their sight vocabulary they need to be able to break them down into separate syllables, like **Man-ches-ter**; or sounds, like **d-o-g**. This strategy is making use of their phonic knowledge. Phonics is the skill of linking letter sounds (phonemes) to actual letters (graphemes). The greater the phonic knowledge, the more likely the pupil is to be able to build up the word. Consequently, we need to teach pupils that words are made up of letters and that the letters, or combinations of letters, are all represented by sounds.

The methods used to teach phonics will depend on the school where you work, but the National Literacy Strategy's *Progression in Phonics*, published by the DfEE in 1999, recommends a system that is commonly used in schools. It also emphasises the importance of helping pupils develop phonological awareness (being able to hear and identify sounds in *spoken* words). It is likely that you will need to assist some pupils on programmes to develop phonological awareness as well as phonics. Pupils with poor phonological awareness will inevitably have problems learning phonics. They need to be able to:

- listen;
- tap out or clap to a rhythm;
- recognise words that rhyme;
- recognise the onset and rime of a word – e.g. in the word **hug, h** is the onset and **ug** is the rime; in the word **slug, sl** is the onset and **ug** is the rime and so on;
- break words down in to syllables – **Liv-er-pool, play-time** etc.;
- segment words into phonemes – **map** is **m-a-p, shop** is **sh-o-p** etc.;
- blend phonemes into words; e.g. **c-a-t** is **cat.**

The development of phonological skills is essential to equip pupils with the knowledge to learn phonics. It is a good idea to check out these skills with older pupils since some pupils at later key stages may still need to be taught them. To be effective in supporting pupils in reading their books you must encourage them to use all of these strategies.

FOOD FOR THOUGHT

Listening to Jimmy reading his book

Hello, Jimmy. Nice to see you.
Let's look at your book. This looks interesting. What is the title? What do you think it is going to be about?
Let's look at the first page. Here is a picture. Tell me what you see. Who are these people? What are they doing? Do you like ice cream – do you see the ice cream in the picture? What do you think will happen next? Are there any questions you want to ask me about this page?

It is a good idea for you to read the text first, modelling how to read as you go along by following the words with your finger from left to right. At the end of each page ask Jimmy to retell what has happened and then ask him to predict what may happen on the next page.

When Jimmy reads, he may need to point to each word as he reads. When he gets stuck on a word, encourage him to use the most appropriate strategy to discover the word. Do you need to ask him to refer to the picture or guess what the word is from the text? Is it a word he can build up using his phonological skills? It may be useful to repeat the sentence to give a pupil further support in guessing the correct word. Skilled listening to readers enables you to find out areas of weakness.

Often, just reading books is insufficient. Some children will need to work with additional resources to develop their reading strategies. Below is a short list of materials drawn from the huge array available to your school.

Using picture cues

Picture cues

LDA catalogue (Phone: 01945 463441 for Customer Services)
Photo cards
Life cycle sequences
And then? sequences
Language cards
Why? Because cards
What would you do? cards
Tell about it
What's wrong? cards
Sequential thinking cards

Learning Materials Ltd catalogue (Phone: 01902 454026 for Customer Services)
Sequencing stories
Oral comprehension
Think about it

Easylearn catalogue (Phone: 01636 830240 for Customer Services)
What can you see?
Order, order
What's it about?

Developing a sight vocabulary

Sight vocabulary

LDA catalogue
My word bank
Magnetic key words
Word building box

Learning Materials Ltd catalogue
Helper books
Working with essential words

Easylearn catalogue
Out of sight range
Word cards from the NLS
Word games

Teaching pupils to make use of context cues

Context cues

LDA catalogue
Reading comprehension workcards

Learning Materials Ltd catalogue
Cloze pegs
Picture Qs
Reading for meaning

Easylearn catalogue
Reading roundabout
Reading roundabout 2
Read back, read on
What's it about?

Teaching phonological awareness

Phonological awareness

LDA catalogue
Phonic rhyme time
Sound beginnings
Rhyme and alliteration picture cards
Onset and rime word builder

Learning Materials Ltd catalogue
New sound lotto
Listen and colour

Easylearn catalogue
Time to rime
Phonic rime time
Rime cards

Teaching phonics

Phonics

LDA catalogue
Alphabet fans
Alphabet cards
Initial letter sounds objects bag
Phonic flicker books
CVC word builder magnetic phonics
Brickworks word building games
Paper chains phonics

Learning Materials Ltd catalogue
Phonic lotto games
New phonic blending (tapes)
Breaking the code (tapes)
Bpd games
Bpd workbooks

Easylearn catalogue.
Phonic dictation
Phonics books 1–9
Phonic ladders
Match it phonics
Which word phonics software
Phonics posters
First letters lines

As you can see, there is a lot more to hearing pupils read than just sitting back and listening. The way a child reads gives us much valuable information about their literacy development. That needs to be taken into account when planning their literacy programme.

Chapter 7
Spelling and writing – how to help

Spelling

Spelling test

1. bote
2. scool
3. frend
4. wos
5. wen
6. bac
7. sed
8. shel

Spelling is an important skill which affects a pupil's confidence with writing. Poor spelling skills inhibit the creative flow of writing. Poor spellers will use simple words they can spell rather than the more complex words they would like to use. Poor spellers therefore often make reluctant writers.

Knowledge of phonics is an important element of learning to spell but not all words can be spelled using this method. For example, someone with a good phonic knowledge could spell 'boat' easily. They would know that it was 'b' and 'oa' and 't'. However, the word 'because' is a different kettle of fish. Like many others in the English language, it cannot be worked out simply by using phonic knowledge.

Often pupils who are poor spellers rely too much on phonics for their spelling. Take this passage written by Ben, aged 10.

> *won day I went to se my nan and she asted me wy I wos*
> *not at scool I sed I wontid to play futball but I did not hav*
> *the rite kit sow I ad to go hom she giv me a choclat I luv*
> *me nan she sed wot a gud boy I am wen I say tankyu*

Ben is confused and needs practice to build up his limited spelling skills. He needs to continue to work on his phonic knowledge, which is clearly limited, even though it is the method he is relying on to work out spellings. In addition, he needs to become aware of word patterns using onset and rime so that he can recognise the shape of words.

The Look, Say, Cover, Write, Check method would be most useful here. This requires the child to look at the word, say it, cover up the word, write the word and finally check to see if it is correct.

Here is a list of example words to develop onset and rime skills.

ad	ee	ight	ove
h-ad	b-ee	n-ight	l-ove
s-ad	s-ee	t-ight	sh-ove
d-ad	tr-ee	fl-ight	d-ove
gl-ad	fl-ee	r-ight	ab-ove
cl-ad	sh-e	l-ight	gl-ove

There is 'a rat'
in separate.

The words above each fit into word families, but some words stand alone and can't be taught in this way. Take these words which often cause problems for poor readers: because, said.

One method for dealing with such words is to use mnemonics (memory aids) which provide a sentence to help the child remember how to spell a word. For example; 'because' could be remembered with the sentence 'Big elephants can't always use small exits.' 'Said' might be remembered using 'Save animals in danger.' There are many more. Pupils should be encouraged to devise their own mnemonics and to illustrate them with a picture when possible.

Other useful ways to teach spellings include the following:

- Giving pupils plastic letters and asking them to spell words with these.
- Tracing words in the air.
- Asking pupils to scan texts to find word families. For example: 'Highlight all the words you find that end in "ight" then after five minutes make a list and we will see who has managed to find the most.'

When has a hen.
What has a hat.

It is also important to provide spellings to support pupils while they are working. The National Literacy Strategy word list should be available for all to see, either displayed on the classroom wall or provided as individual word lists. It is useful to prepare word lists for specific topics. For example, if you know the science lesson is to be on the subject of flowers, prepare a list of words that includes petals, stamens, leaves, pollen and so on.

Older pupils should be taught how to use a dictionary. Younger pupils and struggling pupils should keep a personal dictionary. They can write down unknown words to build up their own personal word bank.

When children ask you for a word, get them to write it down while you say the letters. By doing this, they write it correctly themselves, the first step to spelling it.

We need to help pupils to become independent spellers either by teaching them strategies or providing them with support to enable them to look for words themselves.

Teaching the use of the computer spell checker is also useful, but beware. The computer cannot distinguish between alternative spellings. For example, a sentence such as 'I want you to cut my hare' is perfectly acceptable to the computer but, probably, not what the child who wrote the sentence meant.

There are many useful spelling resources, some of which are listed below:

LDA catalogue
Spelling completion books
Spelling through the literacy hour.
Look, say, cover, write, check
Keyword spelling books
A hand for spelling word bank
ACE spelling dictionary
ACE spelling activities

Learning Materials Ltd catalogue
Daily diary for reading and spelling
Support for basic spelling
Working with essential words
500 word book

Easylearn catalogue
Spelling software

Writing

Problems in this area are affected by:

- spelling;
- handwriting;
- phonics;
- spoken vocabulary;
- knowledge of grammar.

For pupils for whom English is a second language, limited spoken and written vocabulary is an additional factor.

You will soon realise where problems lie. Take this piece of work, for example, from a pupil in Year 7:

> *my family one day me dad went to get me a bag of cips from the sop but he dropt the bag and it bost and the dog likt the chip and it wos not fer and I ad no tea*

This writing reflects problems with a limited spoken vocabulary, spelling, phonic skills, grammatical awareness, sequencing skills and sentence construction.

In this case start by teaching how to produce a single independent sentence, bearing in mind that if the child's spoken vocabulary is limited we can't expect a high standard of writing. If Ben is unable to speak in whole sentences, then he is unlikely to be able to write in them. It is important for Ben to listen to the rest of his class, who can model language for him. Exposure to rich language is very helpful and is the best way for him to learn.

So before pupils write anything, get them to say the sentence. Writing a daily diary with just one sentence is good practice. Ensure pupils begin each sentence with a capital letter and end with a full stop. Once this has been achieved you can go on to teach short story writing, always encouraging the child to talk through the story before they write it down.

Below is a list of writing skill resources:

LDA
Stile literacy materials (various)

Learning materials Ltd catalogue

Writing sentences

Finish the story

Picture Qs

Easylearn catalogue

Single sentences

Write about the picture

Animal outlines

The write reason

Stop it

Story frames

Reading roundabout

Chapter 8
The paperwork –
IEPs, reports and the rest

I ndividual

E ducation

P lans must be

S M A R T

S mart

M easurable

A ttainable

R ealistic

T ime targeted

The Individual Education Plan (IEP) is a key document for your work. The IEP targets should be SMART (S–specific, M–measurable, A–achievable, R–realistic, T–time targeted). It should be clear who does what, when and how.

The IEP is central to the success of the SEN process. It is through the targets on it that we can focus on a pupil's needs and set up review meetings, enabling us to check the pupil's progress (or lack of it).

The quality of the IEP is important but, of course, it won't be worth the paper it is written on if the school fails to provide the circumstances and resources necessary to deliver it. I speak from bitter experience after having worked with pupils in freezing corridors with endless distractions. If you find yourself in a similar situation, ask for something to be done since this will affect the quality of your work.

Devising the IEP

Usually the teacher and SENCo will devise the first IEP, taking the parents' views into account. The IEP follows careful assessments of the pupil, and the targets are based on the pupil's individual needs. The parents' agreed contribution is often written into the IEP. However, once you begin working with the child towards achieving the targets, your views for any follow-up IEPs should be considered.

If a pupil moves on to School Action Plus, when a visiting professional becomes involved, you may receive training regarding the work to be carried out. For example, a specialist from the Hearing Impaired Unit may provide training for all involved regarding the use of hearing aids, or an educational psychologist may show you how to administer a particular programme of work.

The SENCo is also important and should be available to you on a day-to-day basis if you need advice and support. However, the teacher is crucial in helping to devise and deliver the IEP. Teachers are responsible for the organisational aspects: which pupils need your help most, where you are to work, that you have the appropriate reading book, that the work is differentiated and that you are included in the planning. These are only a few of the things the teacher needs to consider.

All schools and LEAs have their own ideas about what an IEP should look like. On page 51 we provide a fairly typical example.

Records

Izzy enjoyed today, but she needs a lot of practice with learning the names of letters. She knows twelve. Tomorrow we must work on c and s.

Keeping records

You now have the IEP and are clear about what your role is regarding a particular pupil. You should also have a timetable; many TAs find they are working with several pupils, groups and classes throughout the week. It is very important that you are on time for lessons since late arrivals in the classroom are disruptive.

The class teacher and SENCo will have copies of your timetable so that you can always be located easily. Checking the hours on your timetable is an efficient way of ensuring pupils with statements are being allocated their recommended amount of TA time.

It is essential that you keep accurate and informative records for the pupils who have IEPs. Reasons for this include the following:

- ⊙ For your own information and as a reminder about what difficulties you observe in one session, so that you can plan effectively for your next session.
- ⊙ For the class teacher, who needs to be kept informed of what is happening; this information should inform future plans for the pupil.
- ⊙ For the SENCo, who will also need to monitor what you are doing and how the pupil is progressing. Checking your records enables them to do this.
- ⊙ To provide you with the information you need to prepare reports for review meetings.
- ⊙ To observe particular patterns of behaviour or learning difficulties. You may see that Wayne forgets his glasses for three out of five sessions with you, or Heather complains of headaches every time there is a reading session. Behaviour can be significant.

On the next page you will find a form which the teacher or SENCo may want you to use in school to record your observations, and after that an example of a completed record sheet.

There is also an example of a completed IEP to give you an idea of how to fill one in. As soon as you have completed a whole page you should photocopy it and give a copy to the teacher. That gives you both accurate, detailed and on-going information regarding the progress of the pupil.

Record of work for pupils with Individual Education Plans

To be completed by Teaching Assistants

Date/Time	Activity	Skills	Observations	Staff

Pupil's name _____ Class _____ TA's name _____ Hours per week _____

Record of work for pupils with Individual Education Plans

To be completed by Teaching Assistants

Date/Time	Activity	Skills	Observations	Staff
Sep 9 9.00 – 10.00	Phonic Blending Tape 1. Lesson 3. cvc blending (group)	Phonics	Billy enjoyed this activity and was able to sound out, and build up all the words on his own (forgot glasses).	M Scott
Sep 15 9.00 – 9.30	Write a sentence in his diary. Page 3 Easylearn: Simple Sentences (1:1)	Sentence construction	Still forgets to begin sentences with a capital letter. Needs lots more practice.	M Scott
Sep 16 9.00 – 10.00	Matching pairs game using flash cards. Easylearn – Out of Sight pages 4 & 5 (group)	Sight vocabulary	Billy has remembered the five words learned last week: will introduce the next five tomorrow. (Forgot glasses again!!!)	M Scott
Sep 17 9.30 – 10.00	CVC blending game. LDA– Paper Chains Phonics–Set 1 (1:1)	Phonics	Did really well – gave him a sticker. Really starting to blend well. He read his words to Miss Green. (Still no glasses!! – Miss Green will send a letter home)	M Scott

Pupil's name Billy Blunt   Class Year 4   TA's name Mandy Scott   Hours per week 3

Individual Education Plan

Name of Pupil **Billy Blunt**   Date of Birth **16.4.92**   Class **Year 4**

Concern	Target	Criteria for success	Provision/Resources	Personnel
Sight Vocabulary	To know 10 High Frequency words, many, three, these, once, seen, sister, take, water, would, should.	To recognise the words in and out of context on 3 separate occasions	Easylearn: Out of Sight flash cards/games 1 hour per week Precision teaching: 5 minutes daily	Miss Scott (TA) Mrs Blunt (Parent)
Spelling	To spell 10 High Frequency words, when, where, with, little, over, make, too, came, want, that.	To spell the words correctly and unaided on 3 separate occasions	Look, say, cover, write, check 10 minutes daily	Sally Smith (Pupil: Billy's spelling buddy)
Writing	To be able to write one correctly constructed sentence independently.	To accomplish on 3 separate occasions	Daily diary/one sentence a day Easylearn: Simple Sentences LML: Writing Sentences, book 1 30 mins per week	Miss Scott (TA)
Phonics	To be able to cvc blend using medial 'a'.	To be able to read and sound out cvc words in and out of context to include nonsense words	Easylearn; Phonics book 2 LML: New Phonic Blending: tape 2 LDA: Paper Chains Phonics: set 1 90 mins per week	Miss Scott (TA)

Date of Plan **Sep 10th**   Date of Review **Dec 12th**   Parent's signature **C Blunt**

Teacher's Signature **L Green**   Name of TA **Mandy Scott**   Provision **3 hours per week**

Review meetings

If part of your role is to support a child with SEN then you should be invited to attend the review meetings. These are usually held every term to discuss the progress of pupils towards achieving their IEP targets. Your attendance at these meetings is important, although sometimes it is difficult as they are held after school at a time when you are not paid to be there. Instead, you may be asked to prepare a written report which can be read out in your absence. However, it is crucial that you attend reviews if you are supporting a child with a statement. Some schools pay their TA a fee for attending reviews held after the official school day.

School Action reviews

It is likely that just the class teacher, SENCo and parents will attend. These pupils do not usually have the support of a TA. It is at these meetings that the decision might be taken to move a pupil onto School Action Plus.

School Action Plus reviews

Reviews for these pupils will include a visiting professional and it is more likely that a TA will be involved at this stage. If so, you will be expected to provide a report on the work you are doing with the child. If you are unable to attend, you will need to prepare a written report for the SENCo. The outcome of these meetings may be to request the LEA to make a statutory assessment of the pupil's needs with the hope that the LEA will provide the pupil with the protection of a statement.

Review meetings for pupils with statements

These are statutory reviews and much more formal occasions than other reviews. They are usually held only once a year and involve the following procedure.

Six weeks before the date of the meeting invitations are sent out to all who should attend. These are the people invited:

- The LEA officer responsible for SEN.
- The parents.
- The educational psychologist.

From school
- The head teacher.
- The class teacher.
- The SENCo.
- The TA.

From the authority

Any professional involved with the child since the statement was issued such as:

- ⊙ physiotherapist;
- ⊙ occupational therapist;
- ⊙ speech and language therapist;
- ⊙ paediatrician;
- ⊙ teachers from the LEA specialist teaching staff, who may include a teacher for the hearing or visually impaired;
- ⊙ a teacher specialising in teaching pupils with learning difficulties;
- ⊙ a teacher specialising in the support of pupils with emotional and behavioural difficulties.

Each person invited to attend should provide a written report to be completed two weeks before the review date. All these reports should be photocopied and copies should be sent to all those invited to the meeting. This helps everyone to be well prepared.

The meeting

The head teacher usually leads the meeting. The child is not usually at the review but their views will have been recorded before the meeting and are taken into account. After that there will be a general discussion in which the current provision is discussed and any recommendation for change is made. The meeting may decide the pupil needs more or less TA time, or the intervention of a different professional.

It is the job of the SENCo to fill in the forms following the meeting, documenting all that has happened, and send them to the LEA.

You may find the idea of writing a report daunting. If so, the form on the following page is a useful guideline to help you prepare. It provides a framework and structure. The hard bit might be having the courage to speak up in front of all the people at the meeting, but it will be easier after the first time. You can practise reading your report at home in front of the mirror if you like.

On the following pages there is also a blank record sheet which you may wish to use in the preparation of your report.

Review Meeting Report

Name of Child ___Billy Blunt___   Date of Birth ___16.4.92___   Class: ___Year 4___

Name of Teaching Assistant ___Mandy Scott___

Provision ___3 hours per week (1 hour 1:1, 2 hours group work)___

Date of Review ___July 2nd___

IEP Target   Reading.   To know 10 high frequency words

Comments   Billy knows 6/10 words. He does not know should, many, three, these

---

IEP Target   Spelling.   To spell 10 high frequency words

Comments   Billy can spell 8/10 words. He cannot spell when, where.

IEP Target   Writing.   To be able to write one sentence independently.

Comments   Billy is able to write a sentence on his own which begins with a capital letter and ends with a full stop.

IEP Target   Phonics.   To be able to blend 3 letter words with medial 'a'

Comments   Billy is now able to blend any 3 letter word using a, e, i, o and u

Additional Targets/Comment
Billy's target to remember his glasses every day has not been achieved.

What has been positive about the support?

Billy enjoys the sessions and is beginning to build up good relationships with the other children in the group. He is becoming more confident and starting to put his hand up in class.

What are the child's views regarding the work carried out with you?

Billy enjoys working with me, but not when we are on our own together. He says he feels like a baby. He is beginning to be reluctant to leave the rest of the class.

Is there anything which you would like to change regarding the nature of the support?

Yes. Billy prefers working in a group and does not need 1:1 support now, so I think he should work 3 hours in a group.

Do you have any further comments?

I am very pleased with Billy's progress but he still finds remembering words to read and spell very difficult.

Signed   **Mandy Scott**   Date   **July 2nd**

Review Meeting Report

Name of Child _____ Date of Birth _____ Class: _____

Name of Teaching Assistant _____

Provision _____

Date of Review _____

....

IEP Target

Comments
....

IEP Target

Comments
....

IEP Target

Comments
....

IEP Target

Comments
Additional Targets/Comment

....

What has been positive about the support?

What are the child's views regarding the work carried out with you?

Is there anything which you would like to change regarding the nature of the support?

Do you have any further comments?

Signed   Date

Chapter 9
The highs and lows
of being a Teaching Assistant

Thank you for reading this book. I hope it has been a worthwhile use of your time.

This final chapter is made up of a collection of comments made by many TAs working in different situations, within different key stages and in different parts of the country. The comments are taken from questionnaires completed at the end of training sessions, from remarks made by the group of TAs who helped me compile this book and from comments overheard in schools. They give an insider's view of the role.

What aspects of your job do you like?

Regarding the teachers

> I like it when the teacher introduces me to the class in a respectful way. Mrs Jones said 'I want to introduce Miss Day. We are very lucky to have her. She is going to help us with our work. We would all like to welcome you here.' She is always clear about what she wants me to do, and then never forgets to thank me afterwards.

> He seems interested in what I have to say about the pupils.

> She treats me like a human being and always asked how my husband was when he was in hospital.

> He helped me when he heard a pupil cheeking me, not in a way I found embarrassing and patronising but in a supportive way, if you know what I mean.

> She always reads the reports I write, and always tells me what has happened in the planning meeting. The staff meetings are after school and I do not have to go, but the teacher always tells me what has happened.

> I like it when the teacher trusts me enough to use my own initiative when I'm working with a group of children.

> I like the way the SENCo always meets us every week and listens to everything we say.

I enjoy the company of the staff. It has given me the chance to get to know a lot of new people.

Regarding the children

I love it when I can see my SEN pupil has really improved – I feel proud of him.

It was great when my pupil read his first book – it made me feel great as well as him!

I just like being in the company of children. I like the things they say and do. They say such lovely things.

I had a get well card last week from all the children in my group when I was in hospital. I was so touched.

I enjoy making up games for them which I know will help them.

In a strange way I am pleased when a child has made enough progress not to need me any more. It makes me feel I have really helped.

I like the feeling I have when I see children's faces light up when I go to the class to collect them.

Other positive aspects

I like the way the job fits in with my own children. I can drop them off at their school and go straight to my own school. Then I can pick them up when they come out. It's perfect.

I don't have to take home any work like the teachers. When I'm finished, I'm finished.

I like the long holidays.

I like the opportunity to meet new people every day. I had no idea when I started how much I would have to do with other adults. I thought it would be just me and a child all day.

I like being part of a team. It makes me feel valued.

I just love everything about my job and wouldn't change a thing. I feel so lucky.

I enjoy sitting in on lessons and watching the teacher. I have learned a lot myself!

I have learned to work computers. I had never been near a computer until I got this job.

I enjoy the variety of tasks I am asked to carry out – no two days are the same.

I feel I have made a difference to many of the pupils I worked with. This is great job satisfaction. Much better than working as a secretary which is what I did before.

What aspects of the job don't you like?

Regarding the teachers

I don't feel I am given enough praise for what I do.

Sometimes I feel the teacher doesn't know what to do with me and I just sit there wasting my time.

One of the teachers I had was very patronising and treated me like one of the children. I hated going into her class.

The teacher I worked with took all the credit when a pupil I worked with learned to read. The mum bought her a bunch of flowers and I didn't get a mention.

I work with a statemented pupil in science and the teacher does not provide any work for him to do that he can understand. It is all over his head and he gets very frustrated and so do I. I have told the teacher about the problem but he does nothing.

I never get to talk to the SENCo or teacher and I do not know whom I am supposed to talk to when there is a problem.

All of us feel like second-class citizens – we are not invited to staff meetings or planning meetings and we have our own room to sit in. We don't mix with the teachers at all.

I hate it when the teacher does not introduce me to the class and the children just look at me sitting there and don't know who I am.

Lack of time to talk to the teachers and some teachers never ask me how I have got on anyway.

I don't like it when the teacher keeps leaving the room, leaving me to cope on my own each time. I don't like the responsibility.

I don't like the pay structure. I get almost the same pay after 25 years' service as someone just starting the job.

It is frustrating not to be told about changes to the timetable and to go to school prepared for literacy to find the school has a visit from the 'animal man'.

Teachers asking me to do jobs for them when I am supposed to be with another teacher.

I do not get enough help with badly behaved children in my group. I think the teacher just likes to get rid of them onto me. I do not have enough experience to deal with uncooperative children.

Teachers sometimes talk and use jargon I don't understand. It makes me feel stupid.

Regarding the children

> I want you to do precision teaching with the cvc group, then cloze procedure with the level twos.

Too much noise in the classroom when I am working with my SEN pupil – he gets distracted, but I am not allowed to take him out.

The groups I have are too large.

I find it hard to cope with children with different abilities in the same group.

I need to spend more time with my pupil, as she would make a lot more progress. She cannot manage in the classroom on her own.

Suddenly being taken away from the child I am supporting to do photocopying, or some other task.

It is always hard when you feel really pleased with how well a pupil has come on, and then you realise how big the gap is between her and the rest of the class. It seems sometimes that whatever you do will never be good enough.

The room I work in is the library and there are always pupils coming in and out disturbing us.

We have no room in our school to take children to and I have to work in the corridor. It is very cold in the winter.

I would like to be involved when they are doing the IEP for the pupil I work with.

I need more training – I am not always sure if what I am doing is the best for the child.

I would like to have more say in what I do with the child instead of being told all the time what I must do.

I feel inadequate sometimes when a child is struggling and I do not know what to do.

The teacher gets very cross in the class sometimes with my pupil and it upsets me to see it. He gets very upset and there is nothing I can do.

I could perform more effectively if I had a better understanding of the long-term plans for some of the children.

The 'head-banging' part, going over certain points over and over again can be very trying, and thinking someone has 'got it' and then finding next day you have to start all over again.

The behaviour of some children stops me from getting on with the work. I wish I did not have to have these children in my group.

The anxiety I feel when the decision is made to send the pupil I have worked with for four years to the local comprehensive school, and I know he won't cope. It makes me feel helpless.

Other aspects of my job I don't like

I need to know more about how schools run – I don't always understand what is going on at staff meetings and I don't like to ask.

We can do various courses to get some qualifications, but it makes no difference to our pay and is a lot of hard work. Why should we bother?

We should have a national training qualification, like teachers, and receive a big pay rise when we get the qualification.

I have no time to record what has happened in the lesson.

When I supported a pupil with SEN I was only paid when he turned up. He was away once for six weeks, which meant I did not receive a penny.

I have never had a job with a permanent contract. So I have never felt very secure and am not paid if I am off sick or in the holidays.

I am not involved in the planning.

In my school we have to go to the weekly staff meeting after school and we are not paid for that.

I think we deserve more pay – we seem to have a lot of responsibility, it's an important job but the pay is poor.

I don't like being moved around so many classes – I work in a different class every day.

I am never asked to review meetings and it makes me feel I am not important.

I am left to my own devices sometimes without sufficient explanation about what I am supposed to do.

There are not enough resources in the school and when I asked if we could order something I had seen I was told the SENCo made the decisions about resources.

Not being given the time to finish one job before being asked to do another.

I do not have any time for preparation.

National Teaching
Assistant Certificate

Awarded to

....

Appendix

Appendix

The good old days?

The Elementary Education Act 1870 introduced compulsory schooling for all children. The provision for pupils with SEN was not compulsory; some severely disabled pupils were deemed unfit to attend any sort of school and were taught at home. One can only guess at the quality of this type of provision. In some cases, particularly in rural communities, these pupils received no education at all. For the remainder of SEN pupils provision was patchy. Often, pupils whom we would now recognise as having a special educational need were never identified. The children who were identified, usually exhibited extreme difficulties. They would be assessed, and more often than not their education took place away from mainstream provision. The 1899 Education Act initiated provision for children with physical handicaps but it was not until the 1944 Education Act that local authorities were required to provide for pupils 'who suffered from any disability of mind or body'. However, those pupils with intelligence quotients below 50 were not provided for until 1970 when the Handicapped Children's Act was introduced. As a result of the 1970 Act, pupils with severe difficulties were given the right to receive an education.

In 1973 the categories for pupils with special educational needs were:

- educationally subnormal (mild and severe);
- physically handicapped;
- those with speech defects;
- blind;
- partially sighted;
- deaf;
- partially hearing;
- epileptic;
- maladjusted;
- delicate;
- in hospital schools.

(DES, *Statistics of Education* Volume 1, Schools, London; HMSO 1973)

Special schools had been created over a period of time to accommodate the needs of these children. All was done in the best interests of the child at the time but today the labelling looks obtrusive. Can you imagine having to admit that you were a pupil at the London Road School for the Maladjusted? Consider the effect such labelling must have had on these pupils. Educating these children away from their peers in their own schools reinforced their own ideas that they were less capable than others and undermined their self-esteem.

The modern era

It was the 1981 Education Act that first identified pupils with disabilities as having a 'special educational need'. The Act stated that where possible all children with SEN should be 'educated alongside their peers in mainstream schools' and not in special schools. This Act was a turning point in our approach to pupils with special educational needs as it changed the focus from labelling the child to describing a child's needs.

The philosophy of what to do was also in the process of change. Rather than packing the child off to the nearest special school the government began to look at ways of including them in the mainstream. There was a growing recognition that the problem lay not with the child but with an inflexible education system which, far from catering for the different needs of less able children, was increasing their problems. It was acknowledged that pupils with SEN needed extra help.

From this time classroom assistants began to be more involved with the pupils. The job entailed a lot less paint mixing. There was a lot more hearing children read and more taking small groups of children – usually away from the classroom – to support extra writing or spelling activities. Schools were expected to identify and meet the needs of all pupils who had 'special educational needs'. There was as yet no clear advice on what this meant in practical terms but, following the 1981 Education Act, teachers became more aware of their responsibilities. From 1983 training in special needs became available to teachers.

The 1981 Act followed the 1978 Warnock Report in which Mary Warnock estimated that about one in five pupils would have some kind of special need during their school careers. She suggested that one in fifty would have a special need of such severity that they would require education in a special school, or a statement entitling them to support in a mainstream school. For the first time we had some idea of the numbers of SEN children we could expect to find in our schools.

Despite the Act's many strengths, it failed to identify what constituted a special need; and it did not give adequate advice on what sort of provision was required. At best the Act helped ensure that some mainstream provision was occasionally available to pupils with learning difficulties, particularly in schools with large numbers of so-called 'remedial' pupils. This often amounted to the employment of a 'remedial teacher' if the budget would stretch to it. This teacher was usually part-time and had no particular training but learned the skills 'on the job'. I speak from personal experience. Support services and educational psychologists all carried out valuable work, but there was no national system for the assessment and identification of SEN.

The current phase

The introduction in 1994 of the Code of Practice on the identification and assessment of pupils with SEN was a big step forward. The Code sought to clarify and establish national SEN provision guidelines. It outlined eight main areas of special need but emphasised that there were no 'hard and fast categories of special educational need' and that some pupils may fit into more than one category. The eight areas are:

- learning difficulties;
- specific learning difficulties such as dyslexia or dyspraxia;
- emotional and behavioural difficulties;
- physical difficulties, which may be the result of accident or injury, long or short term or may arise from a congenital condition;
- hearing difficulties;
- visual difficulties;
- speech and language difficulties;
- medical conditions, such as congenital heart disease, epilepsy, asthma, cystic fibrosis, haemophilia, sickle cell anaemia, diabetes, renal failure, eczema, rheumatoid disorders, and leukaemia and childhood cancers.

The government recognised that it could not expect schools to take on the extra work of assessing, identifying and making additional educational provision for such pupils without providing support. The transformation of the classroom assistant into today's Teaching Assistant is rooted in the extra workload implied by the 1994 Code.

The Code of Practice also established the introduction of the Special Educational Needs Coordinator (SENCo) and for the first time schools were required to have a teacher who took on this role. This teacher assumed responsibility for the day-to-day operation of the school's SEN policy. The SENCo is a significant person for the TA because the SENCo is centrally involved in employing, training and managing the school team of TAs.

So you want to be a Teaching Assistant?

Want to go back to school again, and see a bit of life?
Want to be a teacher, without the worry and the strife?
Have endless weeks of holiday to suit your family needs
And not have extra workload when you leave at half past three?

Would you like to work with children, as a member of a team?
With reading, maths and spelling, or some such other scheme.
Play with water, sand or paint — there's messier jobs too ...
'Oh Johnny, why didn't you <u>try</u> to make it too the loo?'

If you can be compassionate, caring , fun and kind
Give friendly smiles, and words of praise, to ease a child's mind
Be patient, understanding, — a friend for those in need,
These are all the qualities you will need to succeed.

So, if you're looking for employment that's not boring or mundane,
A job you will enjoy, with opportunities to train,
If you're dedicated, loyal and capable of commitment,
Come on and join the team, and be a Teaching Assistant.

Karen Hudson
Teaching Assistant